The Medicine Chest of the Soul

Dyana J. Rullman-Kutinsky

ISBN 979-8-89043-083-0 (paperback)
ISBN 979-8-89043-084-7 (digital)

Christian Faith Publishing
832 Park Avenue
Meadville, PA 16335
www.christianfaithpublishing.com

Printed in the United States of America

Dedication

This dedication belongs to:

God—and my loving parents [Helen and Henry Rullman] for there guidance, patience, love, endurance and for letting me soar like an eagle and blow like the wind into who I am today. It is because of you—that I am who I am.

Forever More,
Dyana

Contents

Inner Spirit...1

Legs of Life..2

A Sacred Place..3

En Redemptis Vigilia!...4

Truth Sleeps..6

Measure of Love..7

Be Steadfast..9

A Loveless Union 10

Afghanistan 11

Battlefield..12

Unnoticed 13

Your Children Cry (Holocaust) 14

The Heavens 16

Today...17

Circle of Life 18

Fallen Tower 19

Facades..20

The Wings of Life 21

Flower of Life 22

Walk Beside Me 23

Father...24

Precious and Few..25

Ode to a Brother 26

Early Morning Memories 27

Listen to the Surf..28

A Memory of Dad 29

In Flight...30

The Cup 31

The Sea of Life 32

The Darkness of Night...33

Ode to My Heavenly Father 34

A Sister's Power 35

Coming of the Rose 36
Have Heart 37
Friendship Tree...38
Rainbows and Butterflies..39
If You Were a Whale...40
Friendly Face 41

Children's Stories
    Alex Meets God 45
    Pee Wee Teenie..47
    The Force Behind the Odessey................................48

Inner Spirit

Mind and soul are one
Life burns strong within the heart
Happiness will come.

The wind was in sight
In the darkness of the night
And the moon shone bright.

Legs of Life

These are my legs of foundation
movement of my existence
stilts of my house
pillars of my inner being

These are my legs of travel
adventurous over many miles
courtyards, mountains, and many seas
conquering opposition, political retaliation, and fear

These legs softly walk through the open field of life
being ever mindful not to trample
the tenderness, love, and kindness blossoming from beneath
only enveloping the tantalizing experience throughout

My legs are not young, but as young as heart allows
they have relaxed through many a sunset
have become energized through many a sunrise
legs are wonderful, don't you think?

These are my legs
where would I be without them?
yet as the circle of life continues
they too will age,

As the leaves fall from the trees in autumn
so too will my legs see its autumn—someday
but not before they have been feed from my inner being
and only after they have taken me back through the fields

For these are my legs of life

A Sacred Place

I sit here at my table, as the night shows its face to all, half-filled glass of wine, reflecting the dancing glow from the candles. As I peer deep within the flame, I vaguely see a figure so desperately trying to expel with each flicker.

The torment, exasperation, and frustration are, oh, so clearly represented through the language of dance. I wonder though, as I break from reality for a moment. Is that what transpires inside our heart and soul? Do we also have a figure dancing deep within, trying to escape? The flame is its housing, ours is our heart.

The night is so subdued and full of serenity. I can hear each drop of water as it falls from the faucet and bounces off the sink. My thoughts can speak clearer than ever now. It is as if they are sitting right beside me. The low soft music adds an ambiance needed for the heart and mind to unite as one. I pause for a moment, just staring into the fire, mesmerized, as my heart takes that journey to where I would never venture.

The silence of the night speaks out with all its glory. It becomes a sacred place, full of wonder and mystery, a place I can call my own. It is my haven, an escape from reality, rationalism, and responsibility. For in this deepest night, with only a flicker of a flame and darkness surrounding all, the world becomes mine, mine to explore on a fashion unbeknownst to anyone. No anyone to criticize or condemn my thoughts, feelings, or desires. It is a sacred place, and it is all mine.

The wine glass is empty. The reflection has passed away. The flame stands erect. The dancing figure dances no more. All that can be heard is the dripping of the faucet. All that can be seen is the shadow of the night.

En Redemptis Vigilia!

Walk softly into the estranged night
Cutting through the cobwebs of the entangled mist
Careful not to disturb the sleep
Which abounds from deep within

Do you hear that?
The unspoken words of silence in a tranquil sea
Which drifts upon cold damp stones
Scurry

Time is of the essence
Half before the darkest hour is at hand
Present thyself on bended knee
And sweep away this hallow ground of all debris

Garlic, whiskey, cross, and virgin water
Will be the pillars of truth and meditation
Which will bring about usurpation
Meditate you must __

Quickly!
Speak only of goodness and redemption of this fiery soul
For the darkest hour is on the approach
Sprinkle the virgin water like rain from the heavens above

Sip from the water of fire, and feel the clamor of this hallow
Earth full of retribution and power
Sip again, for the clock strikes, imprisoning
All that is evil deep within

The torch of love will burst out of the earth and into the air
Silence now rests on the breast of the earth
We must forsake this place
For half past the darkest hour has shown its face

Arise from bended knee, and go forth into
The restless arms of the night
Truth now sleeps between the dark and the light
En Redemptis Vigilia!

Truth Sleeps

Half before the darkest hour
Retribution and power are knocking at the door
Through the fiery sorrows of deep within
Time is of the essence

Purification will come from contemplation and meditation
The torch of love will burst out of the earth and into the air
When the clock strikes
Gone will be hate and usurpation

Yet

Half past the hour will bring nothing but accursedness
For he has shown his face
With all the evil there is
The time is at hand, full of man's truth

The journey, dark and full of despair
Enlightenment can only come from the soul, yet
Time has been lost through idleness

The screams of repentance
The cries of affliction
The trials and tribulations
Will now mark their conviction

Go forth into the restless arms of the darkest night
Be forewarned of the half hour
Remember, truth sleeps between the dark and the light
Be vigilant!

Measure of Love

To what degree doth thou determine love
Is it through my own capability? If so,
My capability is then determined by the environment
Of my past existence, understanding and truth in God
Understanding is then determined by my parents, friends,
And all places lived and visited

I can only give to you that which you will receive
Others will receive the balance I have to give
Love is kindness and understanding
It is a moment of life, all things considered beautiful
Condemnation shall not fall upon sincere expression—sincerity
Being the most honest realization of oneself

My loving spirit could have been a restoration of your soul, if only
Your soul had the depth of sensitivity
I have given all that I am capable of giving and
Have received all that you have allowed me to receive
When I gave you kindness and understanding
Your return was that of hate and ridicule

When I showed you interest and understanding in your well-being
Your underlying misapprehension would surface
I may have faltered in my moods and projected
A strangeness at times alien to you
But you have been as changeable as all seasons, relentless
You keep waiting for tomorrow; tomorrow never comes

For it is like a cloud in the sky, just passing by
They always do, you know
My heart has been poured out till the last drop
I have given you all that I can__ no more!
All that remains within is faith
Faith being the only constant in my life

Be Steadfast

Half before the hour
He has made himself known
With retribution and power
Time is of the essence

Purification will come from contemplation and meditation
Through the fiery sorrows of deep within
When the clock strikes
Gone will be the hate and usurpation

Yet

Half past the hour will be nothing but bliss
He has shown his face
With all the evil there is
The time is at hand, full of man's truth

The journey dark and full of despair
Enlightenment can only come from the soul
The torch of love will burst out of the earth and into the air
Time has lost

The screams of repentance
The cries of affliction
The trials and tribulations
Will be the mark of their conviction

Go forth into the restless arms of the night
Be forewarned of the half hour
Truth sleeps between the dark and the light
Be steadfast

A Loveless Union

To be enslaved in a loveless union and squeezed of all as one
would a sponge, captive until the light dims to a mere shadow.
Yet to have a silent love grow within for another forevermore.
The loveliness of life hath beckoned midst heart as doth
a butterfly burst from its cocoon for first flight.
To give body to one and heart to another, how
doth the balance fall in the scales?
What doth thou do when the latter recedes from thy
life, like the ocean pulling back from the sand?
The heart dost bear a black hole from which love will
trickle as doth blood from a thorn pricked finger.
Confusion and ignorance are mine enemy!
Love is of universal expression shared by those chosen without
choosing the part, at times stumbled upon without search.
Oh! how thine eyes whilst widen as it blooms like
a rose: petal by petal until its radiance showers,
like soft rain falling on a midsummer's eve.
A heart held in a captive body canst be
nourished; petals die off one by one.
The silent love is yearning to speak out,
but voice has not yet been given-
Yet is one of warmth and fear.
Fear of remaining stifled in nonexistence-
Truth and honesty are thy sword, emerging with a cry to be heard
But at a distance, like the clamor of a buoy bell miles from shore.
Wherefore doth love lead us if it becomes
thine enemy and brings forth pain?
Is not this pain the very same as that of a loveless union?
Where art thine eyes?
Cannot thou see the affliction set forth?
It is of far greater wealth to release the "I" that
lives within than to succumb to it.

Afghanistan

I am your strength--
I am your light--
I am your guardian blanket-
Forever wrapping you in blessings,
against all that may come
Lean on me in times of need--
Always remember, I will look after you-
through others I send you
I am Thee

Battlefield

Happiness cannot come forth
Unless change is accepted
Change cannot be accepted
Unless life is respected

Contentment will not evolve
If criticism is to follow
Yet you call me a rebel of my thoughts
And keep delving into my tomorrows

You go on and on until my mind is yours
The battle is at hand
One side says, "Yes, give in,"
The other side says, "No, you fool. Stand firm within"

I do not try to mold your mind and feelings __
                                                        Yet
You take mine to prove who you are
You have used my lifetime for the last time
It is my sad duty to report to you the other side has won
The battle has ended

Unnoticed

I walk along the street at night
With only the moonglow to guide me
Peeking in alleys and gazing at lights
Cannot one stop and say hello?

The raindrops trickle one by one
Pitter-patter, pitter-patter
As it rolls off my tongue
Cannot one stop and say hello?

My fingertips frozen
My gloves all tattered
The rain keeps coming
Pitter-patter, pitter-patter!
Please! Stop and say hello.

The wind blows cold against my face
My journey is long, and I'm, oh! so tired
I'm all disheveled and out of place
I lay down my body by a barrel fire
Why can't you stop and say hello?

People come, and people go __

Your Children Cry (Holocaust)

Where are You, Lord
Where have You been
I have searched for You
From deep within

My body's cold
I shiver
I thirst
I hunger

Where are You, Lord
The children, Lord
Their innocence prevails
I cry!

What have they done!
Look! Their naked bodies, oh, so frail
The screams
The cries

Nowhere to run
Nowhere to hide
Are You not here Lord
Cannot You see?

The affliction of Your people
For what purpose does this serve
Why have You abandoned me.
Touch me, Lord

So I may see
The glory of Your light
Please take me out of the depths of darkness
Please! Please! Set me free!

The Heavens

The engine roared
The nose stood high
As we headed for the heavens
In the big, blue sky

All was left behind that day
Nothing ahead to see
Only soft billowy clouds
From here to eternity

We soared even higher
With the greatest of ease
As the blue light approached us
Turning into the seas

Suddenly__
        The sun shone bright into my eyes
And__
    It was then I knew__
          God was on my side.

Today

There isn't much that I can say
                        __ to you
About my every day
The wind blows strong within my heart
So fierce at times and yet so soft
The memories float in a tranquil sea
Forever reminded__
                  inside of me

The future__
             shock as one may say
Is like a boat cast upon the bay
No way to mend
No perspective to see
Only a dream tossed out on a reef

Circle of Life

As the snow doth fall
And the winds blow cold
I walk among the young and old __
                    Forever reminded of how fragile life is
                    And the beauty that exists

A babe is born
An old man dies
Only to be reminded of the circle of life

Grab onto each moment
Hold onto it tight
For it may never come again__
                    At least in this life.

Fallen Tower

I loved you, Jim, with all my heart
I loved you like most people do
We were in love, just us two

We went through three stages together, we did
Oh! how I loved that funny-faced kid
When we spoke of marriage, we chose to wait
For the war had called upon him

It was a damp rainy day, when we said our goodbyes
I promised myself I would not cry
I told myself, hold high your chin
For I knew with Jim, the war we would win

We wrote to each other a letter a day
I knew he still loved me by the things he would say
Then came the day my dreams were damned
For a letter came signed by Uncle Sam

It was a day I remembered oh so well
For on that day, my whole world fell
A day of horror, not of beauty
For my Jim was killed in the line of duty

They killed you, Jim!
They took you away!
You won't come back
No matter how hard I pray

Forget you, Jim
No not ever
I'll love you, darling —
                    Forever and ever

Facades

Try not to live your life for others
But for yourself
Do not be what someone wants you to be

Feel what you must feel
Say what you must say
For that is living for yourself

Living for others is becoming them
We were all made in the image of God
Not in each other, for we are individuals

Yet how can we become individuals
If we are a reflection of someone else?
Let your reflection be known __
                    They already know theirs

The Wings of Life

Sore like an eagle
Sing like a nightingale
Your moment is at hand

Close the old doors-
Open the new ones-
Hear the sounds you've never heard

Your future is out there
Just for the taking
Set your spirit free

Reach for it-
Breathe into it-
Life is around the corner

This you need to see-
To sore like an eagle
To sing like a nightingale

Flower of Life

Life's like a flower on a bright summer's day
It opens up
Invites us in
When the evening comes, and the air gets cool
It sends us away

Away to where?
The forgotten place
The place where no one goes
Except those on a journey
In search of their heart and soul

A journey worth taking, wouldn't you say?
To a place full of wonder, excitement, and chance
Which will open your life once again.
Like a flower on a bright summer's day

Walk Beside Me

I think I met an angel the other day
While walking down the street
He tapped me on my side
I looked! I leaped!

Oh! It didn't look like an angel
What with wings and all
Just a little boy dressed in his Sunday best
And only three feet tall

We walked hand and hand
This little boy and I
As we watched the morning sun
Crawl deep within the sky

Then he let go of my hand
and vanished into the brush
Leaving a note behind

"No man is an island
For I will walk with you
Until the end of time"

It was then I knew I had met an angel.

Father

Through the mountains and valleys, some rain must fall
As did my father, who stood so tall
Amongst the flowering trees

The lightning strikes
The thunder roars
I can hear my father as he calls
Unto his family so full of sorrow

I'm at peace today __
                And all my tomorrows

Precious and Few

Love cannot be bought and sold
Nor can it be bartered for silver or gold
Love is a gift___
    To be given freely
To someone special___
     Like you ___
       Like me

So if you possess a love you want to share
Pray to the Lord above___
      And
He will guide you in your search
But! remember
Do not smother or possess ___
      For by doing so

You will encounter a world of sheer unhappiness

Ode to a Brother

With a twinkle in his hazel eyes
And a smile upon his face
He wandered down the road of life
In search of eternity

Life and all its fullness
was his and his alone
Until the Lord God came to us
And took him home

Never uttering a word of sorrow
Never complaining of life as it was
Only enjoying what he had
And thanking God

If only *we* could learn from him
If only *we* could be
as loving and accepting of life
As my brother was with his

Early Morning Memories

Oh, how bright the morning sun shone down upon the sea
With its radiance showering our dilemma
You can hear the whisper of the wind as it rustles in the reeds
Such like the whip-poor-will in the year of mating

The sand, with its coolness of life
Envelops my toes and
Sends forth a tantalizing freshness all around

The distant sea rushes in to greet me
With a roar from the heavens
Then leaves

As it softly ponders the ocean floor on its journey to the great swell

Only to return once again.

Listen to the Surf

Did you ever hear the ocean laugh,
Or the sea cry out for help?

           As it ponders its way upon the sand.

The sea has so much to give

           If only you stop to listen __

                And yet

Like people
It needs to receive

           A little of what its missing.

Like the rippling of the ocean floor,
As it latches onto the sand,
And then goes out to sea

           But __

Always returns again
That's me.

A Memory of Dad

Dad, I came into this world as a girl __
instead of a boy

I thought you would be disappointed __
but you weren't

Remember the time I came to you for help in math
I thought you would say, "I have no time"__
but you didn't

And what about the time you were teaching me to drive
I thought you would lose patience __
but you didn't

Remember the day I got married, and you walked me down the aisle
I thought you would cry __
but you didn't

You just hugged me
And said that you loved me

And then the day came
I sat by your side in the hospital
Tried so much to tell you I loved you __
but didn't

I just looked into your blue eyes
Remember?
Oh! There were so many things I wanted to tell you
When you came home __
but you didn't

In Flight

People come, and people go
Cannot one stop and say hello?
Is life such a circle that we keep traveling
Following a road and never unraveling

Mine has completed a circle, I know
But__
From whence I had come
Where do I go?

Should I be the sea __
                          a bird
To be free?
Or should I just be me?

    Dyana J. Rullman-Kutinsky

The Cup

What is it, Lord
The cup You offer us__
           The cup of joy?
           The cup of love?

Both sweet and bitter__

Is it the cup You begged to pass from You?
Thou never told us__
           What it holds, Lord
We only know
It is You who offer it

The Sea of Life

May the sea rise up to meet you
May the storm be far behind
May the Lord guide and protect you
Bring you an abundance of joy
>Today__
>>And all through time

The Darkness of Night

Only a day away
The loneliness is unbearable
How will it be if you are a year gone?

What will happen
If I am not to know your warm arms
Your shoulders next to my face when we are together
The quiet talks on the phone
The togetherness we share in the darkness of night
                                        And, oh, God!
So many things

I am afraid of being alone now
It happens every time now; you drive away
                              Away and leave me
Or go far away

                              Away from me

I am like a child again
I can't be left alone

                      Hurry

Ode to My Heavenly Father

You are the light
You are the way
I surrender all to You
Every day

Because of You
I am who I am
Because of You
I can now take a stand

Your strength lies within
Your love shines so bright
The doors have been opened
From darkness to light

I will humble myself to the Father above
And live every day in His everlasting love
Your angels descending will show me the way
To walk in Your footsteps all of my days

A Sister's Power

THE snow doth fall, and the wind blows cold
As the trees fight for warmth on a winter's night
THE sun shows its face as a shadow
OVER my heavy-laden heart
THE burdens, oh so capacious! The outlets, oh so few!
AVENGERS are all around, despair on the brink of climax

SUDDENLY, the heavens open up
THE radiance showers my dilemma
ALL things being a constant once again
PEACE has once again found room in the inn of my heart

THE angel of mercy has taken interest and brought forth
KINDNESS, love, and a sisterhood beyond all boundaries
MY heart, once in darkness, has been lead
TO the light of hope and encouragement
ALL dilemmas have been diminished to all___
BUT a whisper through this heavenly angel

This angel being you

from my heart to yours

Coming of the Rose

If I were to speak my mind
I'd tell a tale from beneath the lining
of this flower that blooms inside
and of the love that wants to shine

through foggy windows, uphill climbs, and dusty roads,
I thank God for my treasure, this blooming rose.
But what will happen
If-

I cannot be like the rose-
I'm certainly just as wise
I just don't want this coming of the rose
to forever corrode like rust inside

Please!
Don't laugh at me or tell me it's too late
Don't chastise my shortcoming
Just show me the way

For there is a coming of the rose
Here to stay-

Have Heart

I walked along the beach one day
As the sun was showing its face
I stopped, dug my toes in the sand
And just stood in place

Oh! how warm I felt inside
As my soul is lifted unto the sky
The Lord is with me; I know He is
For I can feel His presence in my heart

I walked and walked with my Lord in hand
As the sea rushed in to kiss the land
Then__
      The sea returned to its mother's breast
But__
   The Lord stayed with me and let me rest__
                  Upon His heart.

Friendship Tree

Two little beetles sat in a tree
One went to the other and asked in a peep
Would you be my friend and share my life?
Though I'm smaller and have shorter strides.

The other beetle smiled with a glow in her eyes
And said, yes, forever until the day I die
The two little beetles went off on their merry way
Anticipating the adventure of the following day.

Rainbows and Butterflies

Atop a rainbow in the sky
Hovered two tiny newborn butterflies
On their way into first flight

One said to the other in a perplexed tone
Where do we go and how do we find
A place to belong in this vast space to roam

With wings fluttering like a leaf in the breeze
And heart pounding to the beat of a drum
Together they took off with the greatest of ease
In search of the place from which they had come

So when you see a rainbow in the sky
Remember the baby butterflies, who
Had the great courage
To see beyond their eyes

If You Were a Whale

If I were a whale, where would I go?
Into the valleys or under the snow?
The valleys are green and the snow so white
But I need to be where there is life

The mountains, the hills—they're one and the same
I need to be where there is rain
For rain is a water that makes me shiny
Like pieces of glass, so bright and tiny

Oh me, oh my, I can't imagine
Living in the woods in an old log cabin
Oh, the cabin is nice but not for a whale
I need to be where I can sail

How tired I am going hither and fro
If you were a whale, where would you go?

     Dyana J. Rullman-Kutinsky

Friendly Face

The can ran off with the pan
To live in the sands of Iran
The friendly man
The helpful man
The man from Siam
Came down from his land
To see the can and the pan
Who lived in the sands of Iran
They all became friends and got in the van
To travel to Disneyland

Children's Stories

Alex Meets God

ALEX: I had a really bad day, today. You know one of those days when everything goes wrong? I got up late, missed the school bus, didn't have my homework, and because of that, had to go to homework room after school. That's what I call a bad day! Boy! Am I glad I'm home. I think I'll go to my room where I'm safe. I like my room. It's full of me. It's my haven. I can talk to myself, cry, laugh, and even pray. You know, right about now, I think I need to talk to God. God, can You hear me? Are You there? I know You're busy and all, but I could really use some help right about now. I'm really trying to do everything right and be the way others want me to be, but it's just not working. I know I'm always coming to You, but You're the best friend I have. You're always there for me. I always feel better talking to You. Yeah! I'm always talking to You! Maybe what I should do is listen so I can hear You talk. What do You think, God? God, are You there? Hello? I'm listening!

ADAM: Alex! Come down, time to eat!

ALEX: Uh-oh! I hear Adam calling me for supper. God, I'm really listening, but I don't hear anything. Oh well, it was worth a shot. I guess You're busy with someone else right now.

ADAM: Come on, Alex! Let's eat!

ALEX: I better go down to supper.

GOD: Alex?

ALEX: Who said that?

GOD: Alex, it's Me, GOD.

ALEX: Adam! Stop playing one of your tricks.

ADAM: I didn't do anything!

GOD: Alex, I'm here.

ALEX: Wow! GOD, is that You, really You? Wow! You're really talking to me.

GOD: You said you wanted My help.

ALEX: I did but never thought—

GoD: You never thought I would care enough about you to talk to
    you.

ALEX: Well, sort of. You're a busy man, God, and I'm just a little boy.

GoD: You are one of my folds, and size has no bearing. Alex, now
    about your problem. You're trying too hard to be everyone. All
    you have to do is be who you are in your heart and soul. Let
    your goodness shine through (you have it) and others will soon
    see who you really are. Remember, if you give kindness, you will
    receive kindness. If you give friendship for the sake of it, you
    will receive it. Always give your best at everything you do. Don't
    fight with your brothers and sisters, but show them understand-
    ing and caring. In turn, they will show you love. If you do all
    these things, then others will want to be like you. You will then
    have great days at school and home.

ALEX: Gee, God! Do You really think I can do this?

GoD: I know you can. After all, I'm God, and I know all things.

ALEX: Okay, God, I'll give it a shot. But first, I have to go eat. Oh, by
    the way, God, thank you for letting me listen to You. I'll keep
    this between us, like best friends do. I'II see You later.

Pee Wee Teenie

Once upon a sunshine, in the valley of the green, lived a tiny giant named Pee Ween Teenie. Pee Wee Teenie was a jolly little feller, as he ran through the valley and frolicked through the heather. He wasn't very big, that is, as big as he should be, but he was a speckle taller than those small native trees.

The winter days came along and were very bitter for Pee Wee, for he lived in a house made of pumpkin leaves. As the days went by, all Pee Wee could think about were ways to be as big as the rest of the townspeople.

Alas! The springtime came. The sun shown warmth all over the valley. Signs of summer on its way could be seen all over. Excitement was in the air.

Then one bright morning, Pee Wee stepped out of his house and set his tiny eyes upon the most beautiful sight he had ever seen. There amid the fresh blossoming daisies and the budding trees stood what looked to him like a giant pony. His eyes widened with happiness. He jumped and leaped with sheer delight!

Pee Wee knew that if he could get upon this animal, he would be able to reach the sky. He climbed and fell. He climbed again and fell. Finally, after trying so hard for so long, he was sitting on top of this magnificent horse—no more pondering among the fields, no more climbing trees to see what's beyond. For now, Pee Wee found a place to belong, atop his horse so big and strong.

He would ride through town as proud as could be, shouting as loud as he could, "I'm Pee Wee Teenie. Look at me!"

The end.

The Force Behind the Odessey

As my spaceship, the Odyssey, neared Mars, I could see Pluto the rock. Adam, my copilot, was looking out the window and saw that we were heading for the Milky Way galaxy. There were craters all around us, and the temperature was very hot. The gases of the atmosphere were clouding our windows. I kept saying, "We're not going to crash." There was no gravitational force, so we had to steer the ship hard. Many times, we thought of turning around and heading home to our own solar system, but the thought of defeat did not appeal to Adam, for we were on a mission of discovery involving the planet Mercury. We needed to find out if the temperature of Mercury was rising. And yet, could we get there? Please, God, help!

We managed to steer clear of the craters, and there was no sight of damage. My cocaptain, Adam figured out that if we head for the rings of Saturn, we could get back on course to our destination. Adam and I were the only ones on the ship. It was up to us to get to Mercury because our communication systems were knocked out.

We approached Uranus, so we could land and look over the ship for outer damage, but the temperature was just too cold, so we went on to Venus, where we landed. Adam put on his gravitational suit and went outside to check for any damage. We were lucky; everything was fine. The next day, we took off for Mercury, bypassing the Jupiter and Neptune course so we could save fuel.

We finally reached our destination and found out the temperature of Mercury was okay, and there was no danger of increase. We both breathed a sigh of relief and set the Odyssey on course for home: Earth. It was an adventure we will never forget. We learned that we needed to count on each other for survival. We then realized that there was nothing that Adam, I, and God couldn't do together.

About the Author

Dyana J. Rullman-Kutinsky grew up in Baldwin, Long Island, spending much of her time at Jones Beach, where the ocean was her canvas. Many inspirations came to her through the roar of the waves and the tantalizing sand moving through her toes.

Thirty-seven years ago, she left Long Island and moved to the quaint town of Sharon Springs in upstate New York where she, her husband, and five children lay their roots. It is here where her inspirational ideas continue through the whispering of the mountains.

She brings to the table a compilation of thirty-six years of poetry and children's stories. Kahlil Gibran and Jacques Prévert are poets who have woven their way into the mind and heart of Dyana through her studies of their work.

She made sure her works brought to life the very essence of connecting mind, body, and soul. One needs to embark on the readings with all senses to appreciate the underlying tone of the words that manifest in *The Medicine Chest of the Soul.*